- The Colonies -

Roanoke: The Lost Colony

Bob Italia
ABDO Publishing Company

3 1257 01448 1286

visit us at
www.abdopub.com

Published by ABDO Publishing Company, 4940 Viking Drive, Edina, Minnesota 55435.
Copyright © 2001 by Abdo Consulting Group, Inc. International copyrights reserved in all
countries. No part of this book may be reproduced in any form without written permission from
the publisher.

Printed in the United States.

Cover Photo Credit: North Wind Picture Archives
Interior Photo Credits: North Wind Picture Archives (pages 7, 9, 11, 13, 15, 17, 19, 21, 25, 27);
 Corbis (pages 23, 29); Maine State Museum, Augusta, ME (page 29)

Contributing Editors: Tamara L. Britton, Kate A. Furlong, and Christine Fournier
Book Design and Graphics: Neil Klinepier

Library of Congress Cataloging-in-Publication Data

Italia, Bob, 1955-
    Roanoke, the lost colony / Bob Italia.
        p. cm. -- (The colonies)
    Includes index.
    Summary: Briefly describes the two failed attempts by English colonists to establish a
settlement on Roanoke Island at the end of the 16th century.
    ISBN 1-57765-580-X
    1. Roanoke Colony--Juvenile literature. 2. Roanoke Island (N.C.)--History--Juvenile
literature. [1. Roanoke Colony.] I. Title. II. Series.

F229 .I85 2001
975.6'175--dc21

                                                        2001022777

Contents

A Great Mystery

The story of the Roanoke Island Colony has three parts. First, Sir Walter Raleigh sent Englishmen to explore the island in 1584. Then, he sent Sir Richard Grenville and Ralph Lane with a group of men to Roanoke in 1585. But they left the island after their supplies ran low.

Finally, in 1587, Raleigh planned to start a permanent settlement. He sent John White with a group of men, women, and children to Roanoke Island. The English learned quickly that life on the continent of America would not be easy.

These brave settlers vanished into the wilderness. The reasons for their disappearance are a mystery. Today, Roanoke Island is part of North Carolina. But many historians still wonder at the fate of the Roanoke Island Colony.

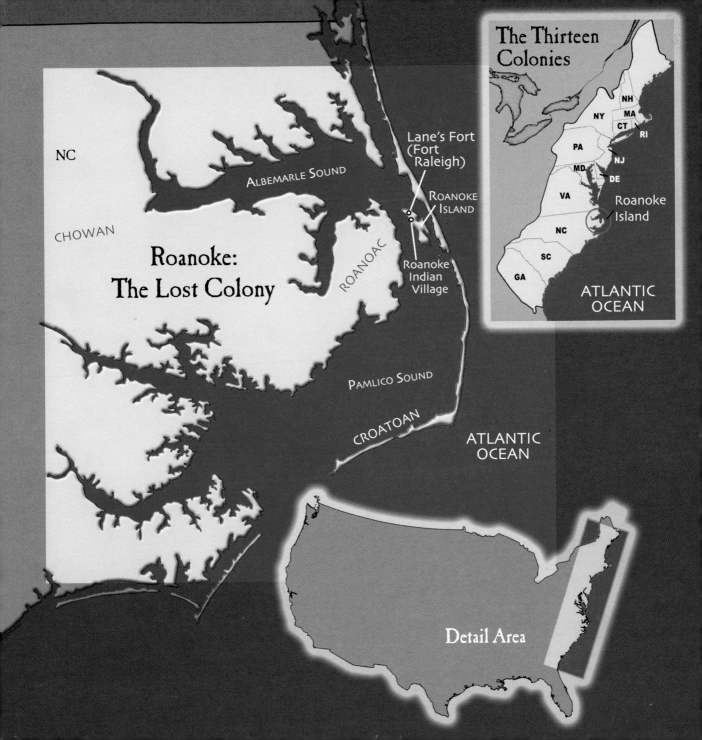

NC

CHOWAN

ALBEMARLE SOUND

Roanoke:
The Lost Colony

ROANOAC

Lane's Fort
(Fort
Raleigh)

Roanoke
Island

Roanoke
Indian
Village

PAMLICO SOUND

CROATOAN

ATLANTIC
OCEAN

The Thirteen
Colonies

NH
NY
MA
CT
RI
PA
NJ
MD
DE
VA
Roanoke
Island
NC
SC
GA

ATLANTIC
OCEAN

Detail Area

Early History

    Roanoke Island is located in the Atlantic Ocean. It is just off the coast of present-day North Carolina. The island is only twelve miles (19 km) long and three miles (5 km) wide. Its land is sandy, with bands of rich, dark soil. The climate is mild, but strong storms often hit the island.

    Algonquin (al-GON-kwin) Native Americans were the first people to live in the Roanoke Island region. There were many different tribes, including the Roanoac (ROW-ah-noke), the Croatoan (CROW-ah-ton), the Powhatan (pow-haw-tin), and the Chowan (chuh-WAHN). They all spoke the **Algonquian** (al-GON-kwee-an) language.

    The Algonquin lived in villages of 100 to 200 people. They built their houses around a central open area. Sometimes, they surrounded the village with a **palisade**.

    Algonquin houses were long. Most Algonquin bent wooden poles and tied them together to form a curved roof. They covered this frame with woven mats or bark.

Inside the houses, sleeping benches lined the walls. The Algonquin built a fire in the center. The smoke escaped through a hole in the roof.

The Algonquin grew much of their food. They grew corn, squash, and beans. They also ate pumpkins, melons, grapes, and roots. They hunted deer, bear, and rabbit. They ate fish and oysters as well.

Pomelock, a Native American village in 1585

The First Explorers

Sir Walter Raleigh was an English explorer. In 1584, Queen Elizabeth I gave Raleigh a **patent**. It allowed him to claim land in America for England.

Later that year, Raleigh sent two ships to America. Portuguese navigator Simon Fernandez guided the ships. Captains Philip Amadas and Arthur Barlowe led the **expedition**. Amadas and Barlowe were to find a good place for a settlement.

Amadas and Barlowe landed on the islands near what is now North Carolina's coast. A group of friendly Roanoacs met them. The Roanoacs traded food and furs for English goods.

Barlowe and seven others took a small boat to the island. The English called the island "Roanoke," after the Native Americans who lived there. Barlowe believed he had found a perfect place for settlement.

Amadas and Barlowe returned to England. They brought two young Native Americans with them, Manteo (MAN-tee-oh) and Wanchese (WAHN-cheeze). Barlowe told Raleigh of the beautiful, abundant land he had found in America.

Queen Elizabeth I

The Grenville Settlement

Queen Elizabeth I allowed Raleigh to start a colony in America. He named the land Virginia. Raleigh sent his cousin, Sir Richard Grenville, to pick a site for the colony.

In April 1585, Grenville left England with seven ships and 600 men. Only two ships survived the journey. They landed at Roanoke Island. There, colonists built houses and a fort. Then they began looking for the best place to build a town.

Grenville left for England after a few weeks. He planned to return to Roanoke with supplies in the spring. Before he left, Grenville made Ralph Lane governor of the colony.

Lane led explorations of the new land. But he treated the Native Americans harshly. He burned one of their villages. The Native Americans would not give the colonists more food. Over the winter, the colonists began to starve.

Finally, the great sea captain Sir Francis Drake arrived in 1586. Drake had been stealing treasure from Spain's colonies in the West Indies. He was on his way back to England. He offered to take Lane and his colonists with him.

After much discussion, Lane agreed. Drake loaded up the colonists and sailed away. He did not know that Grenville was not far behind. Grenville had a new supply ship and more colonists.

When Grenville arrived, the island was deserted. He left 15 soldiers to defend Roanoke Island. Then he returned to England. None of those 15 men were seen alive again.

Grenville burning a Native American village

The White Settlement

Soon, Raleigh was ready to send more colonists to Virginia. He wanted this colony to be permanent. He gathered more than 100 men, women, and children. Then he appointed John White as their governor.

The colonists left England in May 1587. They were again guided by Simon Fernandez. But this time, they planned to settle near the Chesapeake Bay instead of on Roanoke Island.

The ships arrived in July. White stopped at Roanoke to check on the 15 men left there by Grenville. But he found no one alive. The Roanoacs had killed or driven off all of the colonists.

Fernandez decided it was too late in the year to sail further. He refused to take the colonists to Chesapeake Bay. They had to stay on Roanoke Island.

Soon, the colonists began to run out of food. There was a drought. And they were terrified of the Native Americans. White returned to England to get help.

At this time, England was at war with Spain. Queen Elizabeth I could not spare any of her ships for White. Finally, three years later, Raleigh found a ship to take White to Roanoke Island.

When White arrived, he found the settlement abandoned. There was a **palisade** built around the town. The word "Croatoan" was carved on one of the fence posts.

White thought the carving meant the colonists had moved to Croatoan Island. But before White could sail there, a **hurricane** struck. He had to return to England.

White discovers "Croatoan" carved on a post.

Life in the Colony

Raleigh gathered all types of men for his first colony. Officials and gentlemen came to gain wealth. They explored, hoping to find gold and copper.

Military men, blacksmiths, armorers, shoemakers, and basketmakers came to help establish the colony. There were also brickmakers, carpenters, and thatchers. Some men were experts at building forts. But there were no women or children among them.

John White came with the first colonists, too. He made watercolor paintings of the Native Americans. He also painted the animal and plant life of Roanoke Island and the coast. These paintings are the first made by an Englishman in America.

Scientist Thomas Hariot came to find new plants, animals, and medicines. He drew maps of the new land. He also tried to **persuade** the Native Americans to become Christians.

For the second colony, Raleigh gathered families. There were 14 families in the second colony. There were also 9 boys, 17 single women, and 52 single men.

John White became the governor of the second colony. He had 12 men to help him make government decisions.

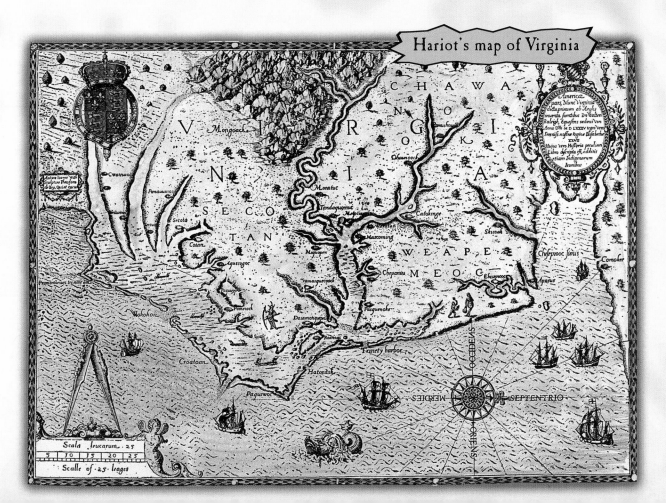

Hariot's map of Virginia

Making a Living

Raleigh formed the first Roanoke Colony to support privateering. This meant the colonists were to stop Spanish ships and steal the goods onboard. This would give England control of Spanish trade.

But Roanoke Island was not a good location for privateering. The waters were too shallow for large ships to anchor there. And the colonists left before they could find a better location.

The second colony was formed to develop American goods to sell to English markets. The colony would provide goods and natural resources that England normally had to buy from other countries.

To survive, the second colony had to produce its own food. So the colonists needed to start farming. They planned to raise livestock and grow crops to feed all the people.

In both colonies, men and women hoped to become wealthy by finding gold, copper, or pearls. They asked the Native Americans for help in finding these goods. They spent time searching the new land.

The first colonists hoped to seize Spanish treasure ships.

Food

The Roanoke colonists depended upon the Native Americans and England for food and supplies. They also turned to the Spaniards in the West Indies for many of their basic needs. By trade, or by force, they secured salt, horses, and cattle.

The Native Americans provided meat, fish, melons, and vegetables. They planted crops and made fish traps for the Englishmen. The colonists ate deer, bear, and rabbit. The Native Americans taught the colonists how to grow corn, squash, and beans. They also ate pumpkins, grapes, and roots.

The English could not live peacefully with the Native Americans. Finally, the Native Americans refused to supply the English with food. They robbed or destroyed the fish traps. Food became scarce.

Eventually, colonists had to go to the other islands along the coast to live on oysters and other shellfish. Others were sent to the mainland to live on oysters, roots, berries, and nuts.

Native Americans taught the colonists new ways to fish.

Clothing

The Roanoke colonists brought all of their clothing from England. They did not have the supplies to make their own. So clothing was very precious.

The colonists' clothing was made from wool and linen cloth, and some leather. The clothing came in a wide range of colors.

Men and women wore a long, loose shirt under all of their clothing. People wore many styles of hats and caps. They wore them inside and outdoors. They also wore leather shoes and boots.

Men wore a coat called a doublet over their shirts. They wore knee-length pants called breeches. Breeches came in a variety of styles and fabrics. Men also wore stockings.

Women wore either a waistcoat and skirt or a gown. They wore aprons to protect their skirts. Women's shoes, stockings, capes, coats, and hats were almost the same as the men's.

Children wore gowns until they were seven years old. They wore a close-fitting cap tied under the chin, an apron, and sometimes a bib. Their shoes and stockings were the same as the adults'. They also wore capes, coats, and hats outdoors.

Colonists had only the clothing they brought from England.

Shelter

The first colonists built a fort and houses. Governor Lane called the fort the "new Fort in Virginia." It was near the shore on the northeast side of Roanoke Island.

Lane's fort was star-shaped. To construct it, the colonists created a square, earthen fort. Then they built **bastions** on three sides of the square, to make it look like a star. The last side was the fort's entrance. One or two small buildings stood within the fort. These buildings held food and military supplies.

The fort was too small to enclose the colonists' houses. So the colonists built their houses just outside the fort. Their houses were similar to those in England.

Each house was one and one half or two stories high. The walls were made of saplings woven between larger beams. This framework was called wattle. The wattle was then covered in **daub**.

The colonists thatched their roofs. The floors were made of dirt. The colonists made some brick, but it was not very sturdy.

The second colony took over the first settlement. They cleaned up the grounds and repaired the buildings. And they built more cottages for the colonists who needed them.

The remains of Lane's earthen fort on Roanoke Island

Children

There were no children in the first Roanoke Colony. In the second colony, there were many families. There were also nine boys who came to America alone. They were probably servants.

Two children were born in the second colony. Just a few weeks after the second colony started, a baby girl was born to Eleanor and Ananias Dare. They called her Virginia in honor of the new land.

Virginia's grandfather was Governor John White. Virginia Dare was the first child born in America to English parents. The second child was born to Dyonis and Margery Harvie shortly afterwards.

Children helped their parents with the chores. There was little time for play. The colony did not have a school. So the parents taught their children when they could.

Virginia Dare's baptism

Native Americans

The first Native Americans to meet the English were Roanoacs. They greeted captains Amadas and Barlowe with friendliness. They gave the Englishmen food and shelter. They also dried their wet clothing. Barlowe reported to England that the Native Americans were kind and generous.

In the first colony, Governor Lane depended on the Native Americans to feed his men. The Native Americans gave the colonists corn, fish, and game. Lane also used the Native Americans to help him explore for gold, pearls, and copper.

Lane kidnapped the Chowan leader named Menatonon (men-ah-toh-non). He asked Menatonon many questions about the land's riches. Lane eventually released Menatonon. Then he held Menatonon's young son Skiko (SKEE-koh) prisoner for several months.

Lane and his soldiers murdered Wingina (win-jin-ah), King of the Roanoacs. His family had been generous to Barlowe and Amadas. After one year, the once friendly Native Americans were angry. They refused to help the English find food.

When White returned to Roanoke Island in 1587, the Native Americans were wary. Manteo **persuaded** the Croatoans to give the colonists food and assistance. But after a misunderstanding, the colonists attacked the Croatoans. The colonists had lost their only friends in the new land.

At first, the Native Americans were generous with their food.

The Lost Colonies

For many years, **archaeologists** (ark-ee-AH-lo-gists) and historians have investigated these lost colonies. They have discovered **artifacts** and lost documents. They have even found another lost colony.

People have many different theories about the Roanoke colonists' fate. Many believe they went to live with Native Americans. Jamestown colonists saw a boy with blond hair with the Native Americans. The Powhatan chief said that some Roanoke colonists lived in his village. But he also claimed that his tribe had killed many English.

More recently, scientists have found **evidence** that North Carolina suffered a terrible drought when the colonists arrived. They did this by studying tree rings.

Roanoke was not England's only lost American colony. In 1607, English colonists came to Popham Beach in Maine. It was England's first attempt to start a colony in New England.

George Popham was the colony's president. But he died in 1608. Then Raleigh Gilbert took command. But soon afterwards, Gilbert received news from England that his brother had died. So in the fall of 1608, the Maine colonists returned to England.

Until 1994, the exact site of the Popham Colony was unknown. But then **archaeologists** found the remains of the settlement storehouse. Today, they are restoring the site to its important place in history. Scientists have also preserved the remains of Lane's fort on Roanoke Island. It is called the Fort Raleigh National Historic Site.

Archaeologists unearth the storehouse from the Popham Colony (above). Tree rings (left) reveal information about a drought at the Roanoke Colony.

TIMELINE

1584
March - Queen Elizabeth I grants Raleigh a patent to colonize new lands
April - Captains Amadas and Barlowe depart for North America
July - Captains Amadas and Barlowe arrive at the North American coast

1585
April - Raleigh sends Grenville on a second expedition to North America
July - Colonists settle on Roanoke Island
August - Grenville leaves the colony to return to England; colonists
    complete fort

1586
June - Drake rescues colonists and sets sail for England

1587
May - Raleigh sends White on third expedition to North America
July - Colonists arrive in North America
August - White returns to England

1590
August - White arrives at the site of the Roanoke settlement; colonists
    have disappeared

Glossary

Algonquian - a family of Native American languages spoken from Labrador, Canada, to the Carolinas and westward into the Great Plains.

archaeologist - one who studies the remains of people and activities from ancient times.

artifact - anything made by human skill or work from a long time ago.

bastion - part of a fort that projects out from the main structure.

daub - a claylike material used to cover walls.

evidence - proof.

expedition - a journey taken for a special purpose.

hurricane - a tropical storm with high winds, rain, thunder, and lightning.

palisade - a fence of strong stakes placed closely together and set firmly into the ground.

patent - a document granting a right or a privilege.

persuade - to move by argument to a belief or action.

Web Sites

The Roanoke Voyages: A Mystery Story for Young People
http://www.nps.gov/fora/children.htm
Learn more details and mysterious information about Roanoke on this site from the Fort Raleigh National Historic Site.

The Lost Colony of Roanoke: A Mystery in History
http://tqjunior.thinkquest.org/3826/index.html
Sparky the computer guides guests through the events of the Lost Colony. Maps, biographies of important people, and interesting theories also make this site from Thinkquest Junior worth visiting.

These sites are subject to change. Go to your favorite search engine and type in Roanoke Colony for more sites.

Index